What Research Says to the Teacher

The Computer and Education

SECOND EDITION

by Marvin N. Tolman and Ruel A. Allred

nea **PROFESSIONAL LIBRARY**
National Education Association
Washington, D.C.

LB
1028.43
.T63
1991

Copyright © 1991, 1984
National Education Association of the United States

Printing History
 FIRST EDITION: September 1984
 Second Printing: February 1987
 SECOND EDITION: September 1991

Note

The opinions expressed in this publication should not be construed as representing the policy or position of the National Education Association. Materials published by the NEA Professional Library are intended to be discussion documents for teachers who are concerned with specialized interests of the profession.

Library of Congress Cataloging-in-Publication Data

Tolman, Marvin N.
 The computer and education / by Marvin N. Tolman and Ruel A. Allred. — 2nd ed.
  p. cm—(What research says to the teacher)
 Includes bibliographical references (p.).
 ISBN 0-8106-1090-6
 1. Education—United States—Data processing. I. Allred, Ruel A. II. Title. III. Series.
 LB1028.43.T63 1991
 370'.0285'4—dc20
                                          91-8161
                                          CIP

CONTENTS

INTRODUCTION 5

AVAILABILITY AND USE 6
    Past Availability and Use 6
    Current Availability and Primary Uses of Microcomputers 7

CLASSROOM APPLICATIONS 10
    Computer-Assisted Instruction 10
    Computer-Managed Instruction 11
    Testing and Record Keeping 12
    Instructional Games 13
    Summary 14

CURRICULAR APPLICATIONS 14
    Language Arts 14
    Mathematics 18
    Science 19
    Social Studies 20
    Summary 21

EXCEPTIONAL CHILDREN 22

ATTITUDE AND MOTIVATION 23

LARGE COMPUTER SYSTEMS 24
    PLATO 24
    TICCIT 25

ISSUES AND CONCERNS 26
    Videodisc 26
    Compact Disc 27
    Multimedia 27
    Software 28
    Quality of Research 30
    Relationship with Industry 30
    Networking 30
    Teacher Training 31
    Computer Coordinators 32
    Effect on Formal Education 32

CONCLUSION 34

BIBLIOGRAPHY 35

The Authors

Marvin N. Tolman is Professor of Elementary Education at Brigham Young University, Provo, Utah, where he has taught computer literacy, mathematics methods, and science methods courses for teachers. He is the author and coauthor of several publications in these areas.

Ruel A. Allred is Associate Dean of the College of Education and Professor of Elementary Education at Brigham Young University, Provo, Utah. A long-time spelling researcher, Dr. Allred is the author and coauthor of numerous works in the field, including *Spelling: The Application of Research Findings* and *Spelling Trends, Content, and Methods,* both published by NEA.

INTRODUCTION

One of the exciting technological advances of this century is the way in which the computer is impacting the process of learning in both the school and the home. An understanding of its role and potential is therefore of the utmost importance to educators as they look to the future. The early popularity of the microcomputer, enhanced by its ability to excite users with novel and interesting games, has given way to more practical and educational applications. Technological advances, accompanied by the production of high-quality software, continue to increase its potential as an educational tool.

The computer lends itself well to the study of many subjects. It can present and store information, motivate and reward learners, diagnose and prescribe, provide drill and practice, and individualize instruction. These are only a few of its useful features with potential to enhance learning.

Of particular interest to teachers are not only the effects of the computer on current and future learning, but also the influence it will have on the interpretation and application of past research findings. Some instructional approaches that have been tried, tested, and proved valid without this technology may not be feasible with its use. Other methods that have not been of value by themselves are proving to be effective when used with the computer. Still others continue to work well with or without it.

Much has happened since the first edition of this monograph appeared in 1984. The past few years have produced significant and exciting advances in the application of computers to the operations of the nation's classrooms. The day of ecstatic anticipation for the coming of the first microcomputer in most schools is now history. No longer is the typical American school wishing for even its second or third computer. Instead, in addition to those used in the office for clerical and administrative purposes, many elementary and secondary schools have well-furnished computer labs and at least one microcomputer in each classroom. Though definitely still in the transitional stage, the computer has progressed from a controversial issue to a rather broadly accepted member of the family of classroom support equipment. We now look to the future to provide a computer at each desk, or at least several in each classroom as needs exist. Even today, however, the practice of using computers as educational tools is not without critics. Some, such as British researcher David Hawkridge, would still question the value of the investment and challenge the rationale for putting computers in schools (45).*

The availability of quality educational software, as well as warranties and preview privileges, has increased substantially as suppliers compete for the huge educational market. Prices of both hardware and software seem to be tapering off at a more affordable level. "Boot," "byte," "bug," and other

---

*Numbers in parentheses appearing in the text refer to the Bibliography beginning on page 35.

computer jargon have become common vocabulary. Educators are learning ways to apply this new technology to the classroom, and indicators point to its effectiveness; however, much needs to be learned about fully utilizing this powerful aid to education.

Studies in the literature clearly reveal the computer's positive instructional value. The purpose of this monograph is to review these findings to provide useful guidelines for teachers. To accomplish this purpose, research findings are organized according to the following topics: (1) availability and use, (2) classroom applications, (3) major curricular applications, (4) exceptional children, (5) attitude and motivation, (6) contributions of large computer systems, and (7) issues and concerns.

AVAILABILITY AND USE

During the past few years, the availability and use of the computer in education have undergone rapid changes that have a major impact on students, teachers, and the educational process. Knowledge of the educational status of the computer should therefore help teachers plan for the future. The information that follows comes from investigations into its past and current accessibility and use.

Past Availability and Use

According to surveys conducted in 1970 by the American Institutes for Research (AIR), 34 percent of this nation's public secondary schools were using computers at that time, to aid their administrative and/or instructional programs (17). Five years later, a followup survey, Project CASE (Computing Activities in Secondary Education), showed that between 1970 and 1975 secondary schools experienced a "quiet revolution that has seen the modernization of school administration and the enrichment of the learning process" (17, p. 9). This survey showed a 24 percent increase, bringing computer use up to 58 percent, in the level of secondary computer use. The 1975 data revealed that 31.5 percent of responding schools were using the computer for administrative purposes only, 4.9 percent for instruction only, 21.8 percent for both administrative and instructional application.

In 1976 Bukoski and Korotkin (17) predicted that by 1984 every secondary school in the country would have access to some type of computer system for administrative or instructional application. The advent of the microcomputer on the heels of this prediction virtually assured its fulfillment. Many computer-enthusiast educators now look for the time when each desk will have a computer.

Typical of America's schools in early transition were the results of a 1982 survey conducted at Palatine High School near Chicago to determine the rate of microcomputer implementation in the curriculum (38). Twenty-two of the seventy-four responding teachers reported they used microcomputers. Frequency of use ranged from "very often" (three) to "often" (five) to "seldom" (fourteen). The most common reasons given for not using microcomputers were "lack of training" and "lack of time." The total number of microcomputers reported in the school was eight—four assigned to the mathematics department, two to the business department, and one each to the science and industrial education departments. Because teachers in these departments received priority in daily in-service training, other teachers felt they were on the outside looking in.

In 1982 the United States had about 45 million students, 2 million classrooms, and 100,000 schools (6, p. 10). Approximately one out of every three of these schools had at least one microcomputer or terminal connected to a larger computer. The total number of such microcomputers and terminals was estimated to be between 200,000 and 300,000. Becker suggested that the number of schools with microcomputers had about doubled annually for several years.

In the spring of 1982 the National Education Association (NEA) conducted a survey to determine the level of computer use in schools throughout the country (79). This survey involved a sample of 1,700 teachers, randomly selected from the association's national membership file. Of the teachers surveyed, 65.2 percent worked in school systems that used computers for administrative purposes, 28.8 percent reported the presence of a computer in their schools, and 10.9 percent reported the presence of a computer in a classroom. The survey found that computers were used at all levels—elementary through senior high school—with the greatest percentage of use in mathematics (70.7 percent), followed by reading (34.7 percent) and computer literacy (29 percent).

According to the same NEA survey, people outside the profession blame teachers for the low incidence of current instructional computing, claiming that teachers are not interested in the computer because they fear the impact of the technology on their careers. Contrary to this notion, the survey found teachers expressing a desire to use the computer and viewing it as a positive influence on instructional effectiveness, job satisfaction, and professional challenge.

Current Availability and Primary Uses of Microcomputers

As predicted in the first edition of this monograph, much progress has been made in the schools in the acquisition and use of microcomputers. While some educators, as well as many from the public sector, are impatient with the rate of progress, and feel that substantial benefits will come only when there is a computer on each student's desk, current availability and use of this technology in the schools is clearly beyond that of a few short years ago. Some daring, innovative programs have used computers to go far beyond the limits of the regular classroom, immersing students in technology (49).

A well-known national survey of school uses of microcomputers has been conducted repeatedly over the past several years by the Center for Social Organization of Schools (CSOS) at Johns Hopkins University, directed by Henry Jay Becker. The most recent study, conducted in 1989, was based on a sample of 1,416 U.S. schools, one-third at each of three levels—elementary, middle, and high school. Information was gathered from 1,267 principals, 1,232 school computer coordinators, and 3,065 teachers. Using mailed questionnaires and telephone followup, the researchers were able to achieve an impressive 91 percent response to important questions. The information that follows comes from a preliminary report of that study, the only report available at the time of this writing (5).

In the last decade, the number of microcomputers and computer terminals in U.S. schools increased from less than 50,000 (serving roughly 100,000 schools) to approximately 2.4 million. Ninety-eight percent of the responding schools had one or more computers, compared with 53 percent in 1983. Sixty-four percent of the responding teachers were classified as "computer-users," meaning they had students involved with computers in at least one of the classes they taught. Based on the 1989 data, the surveyors predicted that by the spring of 1990 the "typical" high school would have about 45 computers, compared to 21 in 1985; the expected change at the elementary level is proportionally even greater, from six computers in 1985 to roughly 20 predicted for the spring of 1990. Most computer-using secondary teachers have at least seven computers available. The greatest availability seems to be among math teachers—about one-third of these computer users have access to at least 15 computers.

Still, the most common use among computer-using secondary school teachers is for enrichment. It was reported that of all the teachers surveyed (5), only the English teachers had a majority who perceive computer use as a part of the regular delivery of instruction. English teachers also stand out as the only group to have students involved with the computer as a productivity enhancement tool, instead of as a medium for basic skill and fact reinforcement. Even so, only one out of seven computer-using English teachers indicated that their students use spelling checkers regularly, and only two percent reported that their students used an electronic thesaurus on more than five occasions. Although English teachers indicated that improving student writing skills is among their three most important computer-use goals, most school lessons related to written expression do not involve the use of computers, even among computer-using English teachers.

Also of interest in the same survey (5) were the number of schools with at least 15 computers—enough so that if the computers were all located in one place an entire class of students, by working in pairs, could be involved simultaneously. In 1985 only 24 percent of U.S. schools fit this category, but by 1989 the proportion had more than doubled, to 57 percent overall and 49 percent of all elementary schools. However, each school has its own distribution pattern. While a majority (56%) of all high school computers are in computer labs, that is true of only two-fifths of the computers in the nation's elementary schools. Only about one-fourth of all elementary schools have 15 or more computers in one room. The surveyors also found that of the computers located in labs, 7 percent of those in elementary schools and 24 percent of those in high schools are hard-wired together in a network.

The Apple II continues to dominate the school computer market, and at the elementary level no immediate change is expected. More powerful computers are making inroads in high schools, however, with IBM-compatible MS-DOS computers constituting about 30 percent of all high school computers in the spring of 1989 and nearly half of the predicted purchases for high schools during the next year. Computer coordinators at both elementary and high school levels reported that the need for more computers, both in classrooms and in lab settings, is a higher priority than is the need for more powerful computers. The need for more instructional software was rated about equal to the need for more computers at the high school level and still higher at the elementary level.

While the 1985 survey reported that classroom use of computers was primarily to provide enrichment and variety to the classroom routine, by 1989 changes in direction were fairly clear (5). Systematic and regular student practice of basic skills is occurring in computer laboratories at the elementary level, while in the high schools there has been a concentrated effort to use computers to help students express ideas and assist teachers in recording and analyzing information. School computer experts indicate that future use will place greater emphasis on word processing at both elementary and secondary levels, with even more growth in the use of spreadsheets and databases at the high school level.

The most recent survey suggests that at the elementary level 21 percent of all student computer time is spent with mathematics and 19 percent in the area of language arts. At the secondary level, 36 percent of the science teachers and 25 percent of all English teachers have their students involved with computers. Still fewer high school teachers report that they have students use computers in a substantial way (23% for math, 11% for science, and 14% for English). "Substantial," in this case, means either using computers throughout the year or using them intensely for certain units.

Computer coordinators expect an increase in the application of the computer to the curricular areas in the next year or two, especially in math, English, and science. Substantial increase of use is also expected in business education and industrial arts at the secondary level and in social studies at the elementary level. Some coordinators report a decline in the teaching of programming during the previous two years.

In conclusion, greater interest in the use of computers to increase student skills is expressed, and actual application of the technology in the classroom is expanding. Word processing is emerging clearly as a major focus of computer-based learning in the schools of America. Even so, at this time, students who use computers regularly at school remain a small minority. For most teachers, computer use has not yet become a major and integral part of their students' academic experience.

CLASSROOM APPLICATIONS

Computers have been successfully applied to instruction in a number of ways, ranging from routine services, such as record keeping and checking tests, to assisting students in practicing skills previously learned and learning new material. Much effort has been directed toward individualization. Although this section describes some classroom computer applications, the primary purpose is to report the effectiveness of these efforts shown by research.

Probably no part of the school is feeling the impact of technology more than is the media center, an area that serves the entire curriculum. In fact, one author reports that the library/media center is becoming as much of a technology center as is the computer lab itself (69).

Teachers who wish to identify additional classroom applications and obtain ideas for implementing them will find help in such sources as Bitter (7), Bright (11), and Moursund (75).

The following pages discuss research related to (1) computer-assisted instruction, (2) computer-managed instruction, (3) testing and record keeping, and (4) instructional games.

Computer-Assisted Instruction

In computer-assisted instruction (CAI) students interact with computers, with information and/or with stimulus material presented on monitors. Usually the student receives feedback from the computer, which maintains some degree of control over the sequencing of material. CAI has been the object of much attention; research has been conducted on student attitudes, self-concept, gender differences, education of the handicapped, and many curricular areas. While not all CAI efforts have been successful (44), most studies reveal positive effects on the factors considered and conclude that traditional programs supplemented with CAI are frequently more effective than programs that use traditional methods alone (18).

Proponents of CAI have high hopes for the computer as a tool to assist in identifying and meeting individual needs. Fifteen prominent educators were asked to share their "wish lists" for education in identifying "visions of the future," and the results were reported in an article by that title (101). Several of these contributors expressed hope that computers would help them be more effective in meeting the individual needs of students. On the other hand, CAI has also been the object of criticism, especially in the pre-microcomputer era when hardware costs were high and educational software was scarce. As a proponent of computer use to relieve the teacher of burdensome paperwork, Crouse charged that "instead of using the computer as an assistant to the professional staff, educators have been trying to make it a member of the profession in the guise of computer-assisted instruction" (23, p. 16).

Many investigations have targeted the effectiveness of the computer as an aid to learning. Burns and Bozeman's study (18) provides strong evidence that a curriculum supplemented by CAI leads, at least in some subject areas, to improved student achievement. Saracho (94) found that students who used CAI made greater achievement gains than did nonusers.

Studying the effectiveness of the lecture and CAI with college students learning a computer programming language, Tsai and Pohl (106) compared three teaching/learning environments: lecture (LI), computer-aided instruction (CAI), and lecture supplemented with computer-aided instruction (LCAI). These investigators found no significant differences in achievement for students in any group when achievement was measured by either homework or term project scores. However, when student achievement was measured by quiz or final exam scores, significant differences resulted, indicating LCAI to be the most effective and LI to be the least effective of the three methods of instruction.

After reviewing much CAI research and interviewing many researchers, Gleason reached the following conclusions:

1. CAI can assist learners in attaining specified instructional objectives.
2. A substantial savings (20 to 40 percent) in time can be achieved for learning as compared with "conventional" instruction.
3. Retention following CAI compares well with retention following conventional instruction.
4. Students react positively to well-designed CAI programs; they reject poor programs. (33, p. 16)

Computer-Managed Instruction

The objective of computer-managed instruction (CMI) is to collect and process information to enable the instructional staff to provide the best learning environment for each student. One basic difference between CAI and CMI is the recipient of the computer information. In CAI, it is intended for the student; in CMI it assists the teacher in the management of learning. Acclaimed benefits include increased effectiveness and efficiency in analyzing performance and prescribing learning activities, and increased time for teachers to interact with students, since they have been relieved of some time-consuming clerical work (115).

Cost-effectiveness is a consideration in the use of this computer application. In some instances of CMI implementation, the equipment and materials prove to be cost-efficient. Studies conducted in a vocational setting indicate that successful development and implementation of a viable CMI system for individualizing instruction is feasible (30). Van Hess (107) reported that a computer-managed learning system in the Netherlands resulted in improved student services, the ability to handle larger groups of students by fewer staff members, and improved course evaluation. Another study compared the achievement of fifth graders using CMI with that of non-CMI groups and found no significant difference (91). However, CMI "was effective in relieving teachers of clerical burdens and the quality of instruction in CMI schools was found to be quite satisfactory." Others have suggested that to further relieve teachers of clerical burdens, paraprofessionals can sometimes be used to operate the CMI system (39).

One of the most ambitious CMI projects is that operated by the U.S. Navy to train military personnel. The objective of the system is to increase training efficiency and reduce the cost and number of training personnel. Scanland (95) reported that through redesigned programs and individualized instruction, made possible by CMI, the average time required to master content was shortened by 42 percent, while the student-to-staff ratio was reduced 23 percent. At the same time, student performance was improved and the attrition rate declined.

Testing and Record Keeping

Using the computer to create, check, and analyze objective tests is a practice that has long been recognized as an efficient means of appraising student performance and providing item analysis data (3, 100). In an early application, Hoffman and Lundberg (48) reported a study of this computer use with pharmacy students at the University of California. In this case students in a large auditorium pressed buttons of a computer-monitored response system to indicate their responses to test items presented visually on 35mm slides projected on a large screen. This system was compared, under carefully controlled conditions, with similar tests administered to the same students in a conventional classroom setting. The results showed no significant performance differences between the conventional administrative mode and the computer-monitored mode for true-false and multiple-choice items. In matching items, students did better with the conventional mode, a result attributed to the freedom to go back and change previous answers. At the end of the entire test session, the computer provided a printout of test item analysis as well as each student's raw score, percentage score, and class rank. The researchers (48) felt that instant feedback provided for the teacher, in a video display at the time of response and in hard copy immediately after the session, made the system an appealing method of test administration.

For another study, Crouse (23) designed a "computerized gradebook" to use with the microcomputer. This system checked tests and provided test scores, final reports, and standard gradebook information. It gave students their cumulative average after each test and provided teachers with an item analysis as well as student test scores. Studies indicated that the system furnished valuable feedback to both teacher and student and resulted in substantial savings in teacher time.

In Wisconsin, the Madison Public Schools used a computerized reporting system as an alternative way to construct evaluation reports (85). The system included a pool of comments from which to select appropriate items for individual student progress reports, thus reducing the tedious task of writing comments. In addition to the individual student progress reports, the computer used the same information to produce a quarterly class report for each teacher and an annual "Pupil Progress Summary" for the permanent records. This minimized the need for interim quarterly reports in student folders and reduced clerical costs. Data gathered indicated positive attitudes of administrators, teachers, and students toward this system, and "overwhelming support" from parents.

Instructional Games

Efforts to apply a "spoonful of sugar" to the "medicine" of learning have led to the design of many learning experiences in game formats. Computer games have been created to teach language, mathematics, logic, physics, chemistry, biology, economics, business, medicine, geology, and other topics. Educators have received these efforts with varying degrees of enthusiasm. While critics question whether mixing learning with games enhances the learning experience or spoils the game, enthusiasts are using the games. Given the choice, large numbers of students opt for the games, and their teachers find that these lessons are "better learned than those provided by the traditional textbook" (58, p. 48). Exploration of this area has only begun. An understanding is needed of the reasons for the human fascination with computerized games for hours at a time.

In a study of second graders, Kraus (60) developed and tested a computer-generated game called "Fish Chase" to present drill-and-practice exercises on addition facts. He concluded that a computer game can effectively increase proficiency with basic facts. Malone (66) identified three characteristics of intrinsically motivating computerized games: challenge, curiosity, and fantasy. Recent efforts to capitalize on such motivators for learning have resulted in the creation of educational games such as *Rocky's Boots* (90), *Where in Time Is Carmen San Diego?* (87), and many others.

Summary

Research findings relating to computer-assisted instruction, computer-managed instruction, and its uses in testing, record keeping, and instructional games, have been encouraging. CAI has been used in most educational areas including curriculum, attitude, and education of the handicapped. In these and other settings it has contributed to the improvement of student achievement and learning rate. CMI has also shown promise for future use in assisting teachers with the management of learning. In some instances it has been found to be cost efficient and capable of handling large groups of students.

Studies of computer use in objective-type tests, record keeping, and instructional games have yielded positive results. Such use has proved accurate and efficient; it also has the capacity to free the school's professional staff from tedious jobs that occupy valuable time. Instructional games have been found to improve learning, particularly in drill-and-practice exercises and problem-solving activities.

CURRICULAR APPLICATIONS

As the computer was introduced into the schools as an instructional tool, some educators felt that it was "virtually held captive by the math department of the secondary school" (58, p. 94). With the availability of relatively inexpensive microcomputer systems, precollege computer applications are rapidly expanding. The findings cited in the following pages are examples of recent research conducted in language arts, mathematics, science, and social studies. Much is also being done to use the computer to enhance the study of other curricular areas such as art, music, theater (58, chap. 9), and foreign languages (27).

Language Arts

As the concern for literacy increases for both children and adults, many are enthusiastic about the use of the computer as a tool to increase language abilities. It is hoped that through the use of computers and the proper application of courseware, reading, writing, spelling, speaking, and even listening and other related literacy competencies can be enhanced. And there is cause for optimism as the computer becomes more accessible and educational software becomes more appropriate to the learner's needs.

A number of language arts software programs have been developed and are now in use in our nation's schools, creating a serious need for more carefully designed research (21). In spite of this need, there is a body of knowledge based on research that indicates the benefits of the computer for individualizing instruction as well as for drill and practice. It also makes grading and record keeping less tedious, and, when used with word processing software, it increases student interest and learning efficiency in writing skills (58, chap. 7). Although computer software has sometimes been criticized for failing to take advantage of its ability to individualize instruction, its potential makes individualization a distinct possibility (21). In a Florida study, Fey (28) found that computer-prepared individualized reading prescriptions were faster, less costly, and more accurate than those prepared by classroom teachers or reading teachers. The computer's capacity to individualize spelling even caused researchers who found no significant differences in their studies to conclude that individualization is feasible (25). Future research can be expected in both ways and means to use the computer for individualized instruction.

Another section of this monograph addresses the use of the computer with exceptional children, but it is appropriate here to identify a few language arts studies that have been conducted with these populations. Weaver and others used CAI at the high school level to increase the skills of poor readers to locate multiletter units within words (110). In this study students were required to detect the presence of a particular unity within words shown in rapid succession. Substantial improvements were evident and maintenance tests indicated lasting results.

Hasselbring and Goin (43, p. 215) summarize research findings on the use of the computer with disadvantaged learners in the language arts as well as other subjects when they say, "Although focus on more complex academic skills may be more exciting and intellectually challenging for teachers, the best research suggests that the most powerful and immediate impact on the learning of students with mild disabilities is through the use of computers to develop mastery and fluency of basic academic skills."

Computer research projects in spelling instruction were among the first in the curricular areas. They include comparisons of immediate and spaced repetition, massed and distributed practice, ways to divide words for spelling instruction, sequencing, diagnosis and prescription, and remediation, as well as for individualized instruction cited earlier.

Knutson (57) found that immediate repetition and spaced repetition produced substantial learning for students using computers. He also found additional practice on words to be more effective than no repetition, and spaced repetition consistently favored over the other two methods. Fishman and others (29) reported that massed repetitions proved effective on short-term performance, but more learning occurred in the long run when repetitions of an item were well distributed.

An investigation of learning rates that used the computer to display correct spelling in several ways—by letters, chunks, or whole-words—found that words displayed by chunks were learned more rapidly than were whole words (9). But words displayed by letters were learned more rapidly than either of the other two methods. However, delayed recall tests two and six weeks later showed no differences in word retention.

The computer is well suited to studies of forced sequence. Investigating the performances of poor-spelling third graders, Robertson (89) found it a useful remedial spelling technique to compel students to observe the details of a sequence. As a result, children made substantial growth in both letter and numerical forced sequence over a short period of time.

Hasselbring and Crossland (42) designed a Computerized Diagnostic Spelling Test (CDST) to imitate, as closely as possible, the administration and scoring procedures of a written diagnostic spelling test. These researchers concluded that the early use of CDST with learning-handicapped students shows promise. The test does not require a teacher to administer and score it and the system can be operated independently by learning-handicapped children as young as nine years of age. Data obtained from this microcomputer-based method reveal it to be "an efficient and cost-effective way to diagnose and remediate spelling problems." Kochan (58, p. 219) stresses that "recent developmental studies of children's spelling have shown that children's spelling mistakes are of major importance to the process of learning to spell." She describes a case study in which the microcomputer changed attitudes towards spelling mistakes and allowed a child to analyze his spelling mistakes, resulting in increased ability to spell. In another effort to remedy spelling difficulties, Hasselbring (41) developed an individualized microcomputer program, reporting that students who used the Computerized Spelling Remediation Program in conjunction with daily spelling activities showed "tremendous gains on their weekly spelling performance."

Because of the importance of reading in everyday life, much has been written about the use of the computer as an instructional tool in this area (103). In addition to the studies cited earlier on the computer's effectiveness in reading instruction with disadvantaged learners and by individualizing instruction, Hasselbring and Goin (43) report that several studies have supported the use of computer-based practice activities for the improvement of both decoding fluency and whole-word reading.

Balajthy (4, p. 78) calls attention to the fact that a "wide variety of research projects have been carried out in an effort to investigate the effectiveness of computer-based instruction in reading." He wisely notes, however, that most of them have been research "only in the sense that they involved untested products or were grant-funded. Few have made serious attempts to gather empirical evidence about CBI or to make important additions to existing knowledge." After a careful review of the literature he concluded that "vintage" studies were still two of the most important. The first, conducted at Stanford University with culturally disadvantaged first graders, found an experimental CAI group to be consistently superior to a teacher-taught group on vocabulary and word-recognition subtests. The second, a commercially supported PLATO project, concluded that (1) more attention needed to be paid to the quality of software, (2) the human teacher is essential to success of a computer-based reading program, and (3) computer learning must be integrated into the regular curriculum. Major advances in both hardware and software could very well confirm, or even change, the results of earlier studies in reading, but the need exists for more research before justifiable claims can be made on the nature and effect of computer instruction in this area.

The computer is attracting attention as a tool for the teaching and learning of writing skills, both to provide feedback as a "responsive listener" (108) and to encourage the flow of ideas by easing the editing process (98). Bradley (10) suggested that word processing can stimulate creativity in composition even at the elementary level. Woodruff and others (114) reported two studies that explored the feasibility of using computer-assisted composition to help school-age children handle high-level aspects of the composing process. And Teulings and Thomassen (105) suggested that the computer can provide information for investigating motor control in the self-paced movements of handwriting. Herrmann (46) appealed for a more extensive use of the computer in writing when she reported highly positive results in many areas including writing, editing, and proofreading skills for those who use them.

In his article, "The Impact of Computers on the Writing Process," MacArthur (63) captures some of the many advantages of word processors and their effect on the writing process, as well as the potential role of additional applications to word processors, such as synthesized speech, spelling and style checkers, computer networks, and prompting programs to help students plan, write, and revise. Outhred (83) points out that use of the word processor also results in children writing longer and better stories, with greater willingness to revise their work. In her study, children with learning disabilities had fewer spelling errors and increased the length of their written efforts.

The computer is a versatile tool and can be used effectively with the language experience approach to learning (36). It can overcome a number of the LEA's disadvantages by recording the student's actual language, being less time consuming than handwriting, and by allowing editing and revisions with ease (99). With the focus on holistic learning and whole language–based instruction it is expected that effective computer–based programs will emerge that will facilitate these approaches. It would be comforting at this time to be able to identify a number of high quality computer programs that effectively implement and validate these philosophies. However, validated programs in these areas are limited. Rather, we find literature that identifies isolated instances where attempts have been made to use the computer in a holistic way (112) or that stresses the desirability of computer programs along with attempts to describe how they might be structured (113). Here also are areas in which careful development and investigation must transpire before valid positions can be taken on the computer's role in either holistic or whole language instruction.

Mathematics

Computing equipment was accepted in the mathematics curriculum rather early. History makes it clear that one stimulus for computer development was the need for more efficient methods of computation. Even though the computer is capable of many nonmathematical functions, manipulation of numbers is still one of its most popular uses. The highly structured nature of mathematics lends itself to relatively clear-cut research techniques and the use of the computer as an instructional tool. Hence the continuous flow of research in this area.

Burns and Bozeman (18) applied "meta-analysis" to studies of CAI in mathematics. They limited their analysis to studies that supplemented, rather than replaced, traditional classroom instruction at elementary and/or secondary school levels, and studies that compared treatment and control groups. From five primary findings they drew the following conclusions and implications:

> While no final answers related to CAI effectiveness or guarantors of success can be presented, the analysis and synthesis of many studies do point to a significant enhancement of learning in instructional environments supplemented by CAI, at least in one curricular area—mathematics. This conclusion must, however, be accompanied by a caveat—that the effectiveness of CAI or any instructional support system will be influenced by a host of variables, some uncontrollable. Failure to consider the mitigating effects of such variables will lead to a wide variance in levels of success. (18, p. 37)

Even before the advent of the microcomputer, a study compared three methods of introductory multiplication instruction for elementary school children: total computer instruction, partial computer instruction, and noncomputer instruction (64). No significant difference was found between the partial computer treatment group and the noncomputer group. However, significant differences were found favoring the total computer treatment group over the noncomputer group. Significant differences also favored the combined computer groups over the noncomputer group.

In Rockville, Maryland, nine elementary schools used Operation Whole Numbers (OWN), a computer-assisted instructional approach to the four arithmetic operations (74). Test results showed that students in each grade (3 to 6) who used the OWN program made significantly greater improvements than did those who used a traditional approach.

The Computer-Assisted Remediation and Evaluation (CARE) project, covering a two-year period that concluded in the spring of 1980, was reported to be the most extensive CAI development effort ever undertaken for the secondary schools of Ontario, Canada (32). One of its purposes was to create and evaluate CAI sequences for mathematics in grades 7 to 10. Teams of teacher representatives and research officers created six computer math courses, basically tutorial in nature and covering about 30 percent of the

Ministry's Intermediate Mathematics Guidelines. The courses contained lessons, tests, and a branching strategy that advances students from one module to another in response to individual levels of performance.

Pretests indicated no significant differences between control and experimental groups of approximately 1,000 students each. Posttest results revealed that CARE students improved significantly from pretest to posttest, and improved significantly more than did the control group. Teachers indicated that using CARE as a teaching aid increased their workload but also increased their teaching effectiveness.

More recently, the University of Oregon's Center for Advanced Technology in Education (CATE) found that students can learn math skills more quickly and cost effectively with instruction supplemented by the use of microcomputers than with traditional instruction. Using the "Milliken Math Sequence" software with third and fifth graders at their test site in Saskatchewan, teachers found that their students using computers scored significantly higher in math concepts and problem-solving skills at both grade levels than did the control group (81).

In its policy statement "Agenda for Action," the National Council of Teachers of Mathematics identified eight points for emphasis in mathematics education. Making clear the association's support for the use of the computer in math education, one of these points states that mathematics should "take full advantage of the power of calculators and computers at all grade levels" (78, p. 1). As the research cited here indicates, this effort is well on its way, but it still has a long way to go.

Science

Computer application in the secondary science classroom has been classified in four ways: teaching about computers, teaching with computers, using computers as an assistant (as with simulations and tutorials), and using computers as a tool (record keeping, test and worksheet construction, and word processing) (58, chap. 11). In the opinion of some teachers the computer is "the most versatile tool in the science department" (58, p. 98). One recommended use is to substitute computer-simulated laboratory (CSL) experiences for standard hands-on experiences for nonscience majors in physics classes to increase efficiency of student time and to decrease investments in laboratory equipment and storage facilities (86).

Knight and Dunkleberger (56) studied the attitudes of ninth graders toward science in an Introduction to Chemistry and Physics course at a Delaware suburban high school. They compared students experiencing computer-managed self-paced (CMSP) instruction and students in a traditional teacher-managed group-paced (TMGP) format. Those in the CMSP sections displayed significantly more positive attitudes toward the study of science than did their TMGP counterparts. And in the schools of Rockville, Maryland, computer use in the Science Career Awareness Training program proved effective in increasing knowledge and interest about science careers for students in grades 4 through 6 (59).

In one study (67) graphing was used with young children to help teach such process skills as hypothesizing, experimenting, discussing, and problem solving. Second graders comprehended and participated in graphing such functions as distance over time, using the computer.

Over the past several years, the National Geographic Society has researched the effects of elementary schools' computer networks on learning and motivation. Across the United States elementary students have gathered data on acid rain and shared their information with other schools. This has proven to be an effective way to learn science, to learn about the power of computers, and to help students realize the importance of working together (52).

Social Studies

As in countless other situations, the relatively inexpensive microcomputer is changing the attitudes of many educators toward social studies application of the technology. According to Saltinski (93), simulations can be used to involve students in aspects of economics, politics, history, war, and issues dealing with science, technology, and society. And the computer is well suited to acquaint students with the processes social scientists use to formulate their concepts—for example, data gathering, interpretation, inference, classification, and observation. As the technology becomes a more common part of the curriculum, aspects dealing with social implications, applications, and impact have a logical place in social studies.

Application of the computer in the social studies classroom is getting a slow start. With a survey of computer use in the social science classrooms of Missouri, Schmid (96) revealed that not only was the computer used minimally, but interest in the computer as an instructional tool among social science teachers is still limited. Seventy-eight percent of the teachers surveyed indicated an interest in using the computer in a classroom support role, such as homework assignments and seating charts, while 80 percent showed an interest in individualized computer-based lessons. Less interest (73 percent) was expressed in using the computer for small-group work. Twenty-eight percent of the teachers surveyed thought homebound students should have access to the computer.

Positive results were reported in grades 6 through 8 at Marblehead, Massachussetts, using software designed to teach elements of the social sciences. Students using the software are reported to have improved in their knowledge of European geography. They also acquired skill in using the Europe atlas and the electronic database for researching information (37).

In support of efforts to integrate curricular areas more effectively, Goldberg

(35) reported success in integrating the use and understanding of mathematics into a lesson on presidential elections with the aid of computers.

Summary

In summary, the computer has been used to enhance study in most curricular areas. Some of the earliest research has been in the area of spelling where the value of such practices as spaced repetition, distributed practice, and forced sequence has been verified. CAI has been shown to produce substantial improvements in certain reading skills, including location of multiletter units within words and use of context clues. The computer has also demonstrated its ability to generate individualized reading prescriptions with impressive speed and accuracy.

Computer use in the writing process has also been effective. A valuable tool in editing, the computer shows promise in the teaching and learning of writing skills. It has shown its value in handwriting, giving the user immediate feedback and reinforcement on letter formation and other elements. Furthermore, the considerable effort currently being expended on the writing process will undoubtedly lead to more research, much of it on the computer.

The field of mathematics was one of the major contributors to the development of the computer. Possibly more computer-related studies are available here than in other curricular areas. These studies have found the computer to be useful in manipulating numbers, drill and practice, problem solving, and remediation and evaluation.

The use of the computer in the science classroom has made great strides as software designed for that purpose has become more plentiful. Students can practice their skill with Newton's laws of motion, dissect a frog, and learn about ecological principles, all on the computer. National networks are providing science students with rich experiences as they interact and compare data with peers thousands of miles away.

The computer has yet to establish itself firmly in social studies. As in countless other areas, however, attitudes are changing toward such applications of the technology. With greater teacher awareness of available computer simulations designed for this area, usage will no doubt increase substantially. In addition, the computer can help acquaint students with social research processes and techniques.

Reviews of the research make it evident that the computer has already proved useful in specific areas of the curriculum. Such reviews also indicate contributions that cut across disciplines; among the most outstanding are contributions to individualized instruction, motivation, and effective use of time.

EXCEPTIONAL CHILDREN

There is one area in which few teacher holdouts exist and in which the use of the computer for instruction is unquestioned, and that is special education. . . . The miracles wrought by such devices, especially for those who have been unable to communicate without them, justify the cost of their development. (76, p. 200)

For the gifted and talented, the computer offers creative minds a new world of challenge, and most studies indicate that CAI involvement with the learning handicapped is beneficial. For example, Carman and Kosberg (20) considered the variables of math achievement and attention-to-task behavior with emotionally handicapped students using the PLATO Computer-Managed Instruction Program. The experiment demonstrated that the learning rate of emotionally handicapped students could be accelerated by computer-managed instruction, but it failed to show that the accelerated learning rate could be maintained. CAI was, however, shown to have a significant positive influence on attention-to-task behavior.

Education of the disadvantaged was one of the early successes of the computer in educational applications. Maser (68) and others investigated an alternative approach to individual instruction in basic skills for economically and educationally disadvantaged students at the secondary level. These researchers used CAI in priority areas: arithmetic, language arts, and reading with students "severely deficient" in one or more of these skills. At the end of a three-year period, results indicated that CAI was effective in building basic skills with these students.

Holz and others (50) used CAI to teach basic money-handling skills to trainable mentally handicapped students (ages 7 to 20). The instruction included basic arithmetic skills necessary for handling small amounts of money. These researchers found achievement differences to be statistically significant in favor of the CAI group over the control group.

Other studies lend support to the positive effects of CAI with the learning handicapped. They include Lally's efforts (61) to help retarded children (ages 9 to 14) acquire number conservation skills, and Hasselbring's study (41) of spelling achievement with the learning handicapped. Watkins and Webb (109) also found CAI to be effective in increasing math skills of elementary-level learning-disabled students.

Steele, Battista, and Krockover (102) studied the effect of computer-assisted drill-and-practice math instruction on the computer literacy of fifth graders of high intellectual ability. They found the computer-assisted approach was just as effective as traditional methods in developing math skills, with the added advantage of developing significant increases in affective and cognitive computer literacy.

Concerned about the high number of young people to whom the doors of higher education were closed, Maricopa Community College in Phoenix, Arizona, greatly strengthened its outreach system to the area's public schools

(8). This effort to help more students graduate involved an innovative computerized program to identify and track public school students considered to be at risk of dropping out. Personnel monitored these students and guided them over the rough spots of their high school years. Success of this effort resulted in over 90 percent of those targeted at risk graduating from high school and over 80 percent going on to college.

Many people hold high hopes that technology will help improve the level of success for exceptional children through increased motivation, improved effectiveness of instruction, and, where needed, greater challenge (104). Potential for computer use by both gifted and handicapped students appears to be great. In addition to enabling the blind to "read" books and the deaf to communicate over telephone lines, the computer has also helped handicapped students to stay on task, and it has proved to be a viable tool in helping them develop basic skills. These are but a few evidences of the computer's uses with exceptional children.

In using computers with the gifted, Brooks (12) found that students of grades 1–8 gained skills and knowledge in both computer use and academic areas. Long-term benefits, when students were allowed continued access to computers in the classroom, included better organization of information and assignments more consistently finished on time.

ATTITUDE AND MOTIVATION

Student interest and motivation are among the greatest challenges in teaching; these elements are basic to student success. In handwriting, for example, practically all new skills have been taught by the time children leave third grade. Progress beyond that grade level depends largely upon the teacher's ability to motivate students. In spelling instruction, keeping interest high appears to be the most essential element (1). This is also true in other areas of the curriculum.

Studies often report positive student attitudes toward the computer and its educational uses, as well as its ability to motivate and maintain high interest (22). The samples that follow summarize many of these findings.

In the early years of the computer in the classroom, Robertson (89) found that children who experienced frequent frustration from classroom failure responded positively to the challenge of computer-assisted programs presented on teletype terminals. She concluded that children involved in the study did not seem to have a sense of failure when they made an incorrect response on the teletype terminal. Rather, they reacted as if they were playing a challenging game with an opportunity to try again.

Attitude surveys about the CARE (Computer-Assisted Remediation and Evaluation) mathematics approach to learning indicated that both students and teachers felt positively toward the system (32). Common teacher responses included "It's a good individualized program." "It motivates disinterested students." "It proceeds at a student's own rate." Student responses included "You can learn at your own rate." "It's fun." "It's a change from the classroom." "It's easy to understand." "No teacher to yell at you."

Studying the effects of student personality on success with CAI, Hoffman and Waters (47) found several traits that seemed to favor such success. They included the ability to concentrate quietly, the ability to pay attention to details, an affinity for memorizing facts, and the ability to stay with a single task until completion.

Among the computer's most valuable potential contributions is its ability to motivate and keep student interest high. Roth (92) and Denny and Denny (26) found that attaching a temperature probe to the computer increased student interest when learning about heat. Research conducted to date has indicated that student reactions toward certain subjects have been positive in nearly every case as a result of computer use. Excited by its ability to individualize instruction, students see the computer as a useful educational tool, which they consider to be friendly.

LARGE COMPUTER SYSTEMS

Computers are available in three size categories: microcomputers, minicomputers, and mainframes. A major difference among the three types is their capacity to store and process information. With continued development of the microchip and other devices for storing information, such as disk drives, the differences are becoming less obvious. In spite of these vanishing differences, however, at least two large, well-known systems—both funded by the National Science Foundation—continue to make an impact in education: PLATO (Programmed Logic for Automatic Teaching Operations) and TICCIT (Time-shared, Interactive, Computer-Controlled Information Television).

PLATO

Based at the University of Illinois and marketed by Control Data Corporation, the PLATO system serves hundreds of terminals across the nation, each accessing its memory banks via telephone lines. Its enormous memory capacity and large-scale computing capability enable PLATO to serve these terminals simultaneously and to offer programs that exceed the capabilities of less powerful computers. PLATO can also produce programs with voice and sophisticated graphics, including animation. It is perhaps the best known CAI project in the world (40) and has been the object of considerable CAI research. A few examples from different educational levels follow.

In 1980 Mercer University in Macon, Georgia, acquired a PLATO IV learning station (terminal) to determine if students would use it and if student attitudes toward this type of CAI would prove positive (53). Of the several departments with access to the terminal, the heaviest user was the chemistry department. Through computerized simulations chemistry students learned and practiced skills, which they then applied in the laboratory. Overall, the abbreviated trial period demonstrated that students did use the PLATO IV system and that its use generated favorable attitudes.

Davis (24) reported positive results in both achievement and attitude for students in grades 4 through 6 using PLATO computer math lessons. And Brown's analysis (13) of a field study at three Florida high schools that used the math portion of the PLATO Basic Skills Learning System in remedial courses showed the PLATO system to be both effective and cost efficient.

TICCIT

The TICCIT system was developed at the University of Texas and Brigham Young University. Using minicomputers, the system, initially designed to provide instruction in English and mathematics (40), is capable of handling up to 128 terminals. It automatically keeps records of user progress and types of responses. TICCIT was evaluated by the Educational Testing Service in three environments: community college, university, and an advanced training school for military flight crews (71). When used in mathematics courses in community colleges, the completion rate in TICCIT classes was lower than in conventional classes, and fewer TICCIT mathematics students went on to advanced courses. For students who completed the courses, TICCIT required the same amount of study time as conventional lecture sections. In English classes there were no differences between TICCIT and conventional sections, except in some areas where lower-ability students did better with TICCIT than with the lecture approach.

Results at the university level were somewhat different. TICCIT students in mathematics classes did as well as those from lecture sections using essentially the same content. English students ranked TICCIT as their first choice as an instructional method, followed by discussion, tutoring, lecture, and home study, in that order. A navy study resulted in an enthusiastic acceptance of CAI training, and participants made slightly better progress with TICCIT than those in a traditional classroom setting.

Overall, students using TICCIT have been found to perform at about the same mastery level as those using other methods. However, students seem to find the system more challenging and usually prefer it to conventional instruction.

The studies cited here are representative of the research that has used PLATO and TICCIT in CAI applications. Such efforts have shown these systems to be effective educational tools that support classroom instruction.

ISSUES AND CONCERNS

As Friedrichs and Schaff (31) noted, the new generation must be prepared to take its place in a very different world, one whose shape we can only guess. The substance of these "guesses" will influence the shaping of the future; the accuracy of these guesses will help determine the effectiveness of our efforts to prepare the next generation. Kibler and Campbell (55) likened efforts to determine needed educational changes to an attempt to hit a moving target—it is necessary to aim where it will be, not where it is, and judge the speed of the target in relation to the speed of the projectile. As they observed, "We can think of no faster moving target for the lumbering cannon of education to take aim at than computers and their impact on education" (p. 44).

The use of the computer, particularly the microcomputer, is already making a dramatic impact on many aspects of human endeavor. Education is one of the areas now feeling this influence and it will continue to do so. The ability to anticipate the potential use of the computer is imperative. To maximize future possibilities, however, an awareness of its past influence and current impact, as well as its potential, is necessary. Armed with this information, educators will then be in a position to make wise decisions about acquisition and future use.

The major purpose of this monograph has been to report data on the educational uses of the computer that have been substantiated by research. Future planning requires an awareness of potential technology, as well as of related issues and concerns. Among the technology already available for use are the videodisc and the compact disc. Issues and concerns include multimedia, software—its quality and protection—the kind and quality of research, the school's relationship with industry, networking, the training of teachers, the use of computer coordinators at school and district levels, and the effect of the computer on formal education. These issues are treated in the following pages.

Videodisc

After several years of questionable destiny in education, the videodisc now seems to be taking its place as a full-fledged member of the educational technology team. Similar in appearance to a 78 rpm phonograph record, the videodisc contains prerecorded audio and video information (such as movies or educational programs) that, by use of a player, can be reproduced on a TV set. Among the features that give the videodisc an advantage over the videotape for classroom application are its potential for instant access to a particular part of a program and its ability to produce high-quality still pictures.

Many educators are now using the videodisc and praise its success (62, 111). Aware of the development of the laser-read videodisc, its versatility with freeze-frame and random access capability, and its interactive capability with computer interface, Schneider predicted in 1976, "it will only be a matter of time until videodiscs completely replace conventional motion pictures in educational institutions" (97, p. 54). The conventional motion picture film is giving way to the videotape, but with the lingering advantages of the videotape, the videodisc is not yet taking a very strong grip on the movie industry. For the school setting, however, advances in videodisc technology promise to carry the dreams of proponents of individualized instruction a step closer to reality.

In 1981 Glenn and Kehrberg (34) identified the key issues for users and developers of videodisc technology as follows: availability of quality courseware, cost of production, hardware selection, and training of educators. So popular is it becoming, and so bright its future that Mageau claims laser-disc technology is writing a new definition of educational software.

No longer is software viewed simply as the little square disks that go into microcomputer slots. Software-industry and education leaders now see software as any platform that can electronically deliver instructional materials, regardless of the kind of machine it runs on. And the newest platform at the frontier of the 1990s is laser-disc technology. (65)

Exciting applications currently being researched interface the videodisc with the computer. The major strength of interactive video is its ability to interact with the learner. Evidence of its effectiveness in improving both motivation and learning is accumulating rapidly (2). California State University, Fullerton, reports gratifying results in the implementation of interactive videodisc on its campus and beyond (88).

Compact Disc

Lurking on the horizon and currently being groomed for a huge impact on education is the compact disc (CD). Already setting the audio world on its heels with its clarity of sound reproduction and gigantic storage capacity, the CD is struggling to break into the world of video. In digital format, pictures use up enormous amounts of memory space with current technology. Video uses 30 frames per second, and an entire CD has capacity for only a few minutes of movie material. Still, exciting things are happening, including entire sets of encyclopedias, complete with thousands of illustrations, sound, and impressive search capabilities, all on a single disc. The same CD can store only about a half minute of high-quality video (84).

Multimedia

Many schools have progressed in their level of sophistication with the computer to the point of using it as a multimedia machine to input, manipulate, and output graphics, audio, and video. A new level of motivation is provided for students and schools to get more out of their investment in technology. Some see the trend moving toward the computer as the orchestrator of media, with more and more devices able to work through the computer. Beginning students learn to make video book reports, using the computer instead of a camera to input information onto the videotape. As students progress in their experience and sophistication with the equipment, they can add sound, including music and narration, and more. Still pictures can even be taken with cameras that record pictures on disc. The pictures can then be loaded into the computer, allowing images to be digitized and manipulated (19). With the use of multimedia, subjects come alive for students, as printed symbols are replaced by moving pictures (70).

Software

Major future concerns facing educators using computers include a need for appropriate software. A survey by the National Education Association in 1982 reflected this concern (79). The majority of educators responding to the survey expressed dissatisfaction with the amount of available software. Many also expressed concern about software quality. While great progress has been made in recent years, these concerns continue (76). Jolicoeur and Berger (54) suggest that one of the biggest problems with software is not in the software itself, but in the logistics of implementing it into the classroom. Other issues of consequence to users include software protection with its implications for purchase and use.

Quality Control

As the first edition of this monograph stated: "The task of controlling the quality of software is of utmost importance. As suppliers attempt to meet the demands for software, products of all kinds are beginning to flood the market. Consequently, it is safe to observe that many products will be of inferior quality. Far too few have been properly researched" (p. 23). Since then software quality has risen with competition and the expectation level of the market, and significant progress continues.

Producers have a responsibility for the quality of their product. But, users exert the greatest influence as they dictate what they will and will not buy. The review and evaluation of software by qualified organizations can assist users to make informed purchasing decisions. For example, CONDUIT, funded by the National Science Foundation and based at the Weeg Computer Center at the University of Iowa, and MicroSIFT (Microcomputer Software Information for Teachers), established by the Northwest Regional Educational Laboratory in Portland, Oregon, and funded by the National Institute of Education, are two agencies currently performing these functions. MECC (Minnesota Educational Computing Consortium), MACUL (Michigan Association for Computer Users in Learning), and the computer program reviews of *Educational*

Technology and other professional journals represent additional types of efforts in this important area.

Software Protection

The illegal duplication of software has become a major issue in the use of microcomputers in education. The way this problem is handled will have a marked influence on software availability. Following a survey of software producers to explore their concerns about this issue, Hoover and Gould (51) contended there is much misunderstanding and little clarity about software protection rights. Respondents' opinions ranged from beliefs about mistreatment of software producers to beliefs about inadequate protection of users.

The researchers in this survey randomly selected 68 publishing houses from among 451 that produce software for the Apple microcomputer. Results included the following:

1. Preview:
    Seventy-five percent of the respondents do not allow preview of software prior to purchases. Fifteen percent allow preview and 10 percent did not respond to this item.
2. Return Option:
    Forty-five percent allow preview after purchase, with a return option.
3. Copy protection:
    Sixty percent reported that software was not copy-protected.
4. Backup copies:
    Seventy-two percent provide no backup copies. Six percent provide one backup without additional charge. Twenty-two percent provide backup copies with additional charge.
5. Negotiability of special multicopy prices:
    Eighty-two and one-half percent indicated willingness to negotiate special prices for purchase of multiple copies or a licensing agreement to make multiple copies of programs.
6. Illegal duplication of products by schools:
    Thirty-five percent of the producers consider illegal duplication of software by schools to be a serious threat to profits. (51)

Hoover and Gould considered willingness to negotiate special multicopy prices to be the most significant finding of the study. They also expressed dismay that so few software producers were willing to allow schools to preview their products; they suggested that this may be due to the producers' assumption that buyers make copies of programs and then return the originals for refunds.

Problems of the software industry will not be easily resolved. Schools want to buy software, but because of limited budgets they prefer to preview a product before investing in it. Software companies want to sell their product, but they must also protect their huge production investments and marketing costs. A partial solution might be greater adherence to legal and ethical codes on the part of school systems to earn the trust of software producers and to encourage more liberal sales policies such as preview privileges and backup copy allowances.

Quality of Research

Another continuing concern is the kind and quality of research conducted in computer education. A serious immediate danger is the possibility that investigators might "jump on the bandwagon" and conduct subquality work. Computer programming requires systematic structure; thus certain questions must be asked when "significant" results are found in CAI research. Are the differences attributable to the influence of the computer on the learning task? Or did the developer use more care in the instructional design than would have been the case without the computer? Also, did the researchers disregard necessary elements of design, implementation, or proper treatment of data? Poorly conducted studies can produce inaccurate findings, causing users to draw misleading conclusions that result in inappropriate applications—a condition that plagues and frustrates serious consumers of educational research.

Relationship with Industry

According to Nathan (77), educators should stop trying to adapt computers to fit schools and begin adapting schools to fully use computer capabilities. His plea includes rethinking the "where," the "who," and the "what" of education. Consequently he suggested replacing school buildings with community learning centers where K-12 programs, agencies, and businesses could jointly use computers and other technology. In such a setting more equipment could be afforded for each group's use than would be the case if each group had to purchase its own. Under these conditions capable, technologically oriented people could have joint appointments between high technology companies and schools. Nathan also believes that technological tools, such as television, videotape recorders, and computers, must no longer be "trivialized" in the schools as occasional supplements to classes; they should be fully utilized to help students create and think.

Networking

A local network joins two or more computers together so they can share information or peripherals. Printers and other devices may be a part of the network. Some states and school districts are establishing centers for storing a library of software. As these systems become more sophisticated, the notion of networking expands beyond the school computer lab. Schools, district offices, and state computer centers can share data and software, where appropriate, by means of telephone lines. These connections provide interschool networks, encouraging interaction in such forms as electronic mail, sharing of locally written software and utilization of common data bases. Certain time-sharing systems, such as PLATO, have been providing interschool networks with many schools linked to the same mainframe computer. Research is continuing in this area.

In an elementary school with a network of 25 computers, students were given science projects to investigate and encouraged to share their findings among individual students, between student groups, and with their teachers. Called the Earth Lab, the curriculum was intended to provide the critical features of "real science." Students collaborated in such investigations as the relationships between locations of earthquakes and volcanoes and plate tectonics, and found how their own work fit into the larger picture. In addition to the cooperative learning that took place directly related to the project, the researchers documented an increase in the use of small groups in various classroom subjects and tasks (80).

Teacher Training

A major challenge facing educators involves both pre-service and inservice teacher training in computer use. Also of concern is both the content and nature of that training. Pre-service needs are evidenced by the computer literacy expected of graduating teachers. In-service needs exist because many current faculty members in educational institutions completed their formal training before the advent of the computer in the school. Others received their training in institutions that were slow to respond to the need for computer training in the professional courses of teachers. Even today many institutions are lacking in the computer background they offer in pre-service teacher education programs (14).

Despite much support for teaching computer literacy, there is little consensus concerning its content (16). According to Molnar:

> In a field where technological change occurs literally overnight and where computer generations are measured in two to three years, what is literacy? Rapid change is not easily accepted by a profession such as education, which usually measures innovative adoption by generations of teachers and decades of time. (73, p.28)

The Northwest Council for Computer Education (NCCE), in cooperation with Oregon State University, identified competencies for use as guidelines in the computer training of both in-service and pre-service teachers. With input from specialists at all levels, this group recommended specific competencies for each category of personnel, including classroom teachers, computer teachers, and computer coordinators at elementary, middle school, and high school levels (82). The actual list of competencies recommended is much too comprehensive to itemize here, but as examples, keyboarding skills were regarded as necessary at all levels, "the earlier the better." Programming was considered important only for teachers directly involved with it and was quickly removed from the list for the general classroom teacher. The teaching of programming was recognized as important for the high school level and therefore a skill needed by high school computer teachers. It was regarded as "OK to know it, but you won't teach much of it" at the middle school level, and outdated at the elementary level, "appropriate in the 70s and early 80s but no longer."

Computer Coordinators

An increasing number of computer coordinators are being assigned at all levels. Their tasks usually include hardware maintenance, recommending hardware and software, evaluating hardware and software, and training teachers, as well as teaching students. Bruder (15) surveyed district- and school-level coordinators nationwide. On the positive side, she found that the majority of computer coordinators, at both the school and district levels, report that they are either "satisfied" or "more than satisfied" with their work. Their primary obstacles are time and money. The typical computer coordinator is in his or her early forties and teaches in the public schools in addition to carrying out the duties of computer coordinator. Sixty-four percent of all computer coordinators work in that role only part-time. Fifty-nine percent of the part-time coordinators are male and more than half receive no additional compensation. On the other hand, among full-time computer coordinators, females outnumber males by 13 percent. Major shifts in responsibilities from 1987 to 1989 included more time devoted to hardware. During the same period, the proportion of computer coordinators teaching programming skills to students decreased from 70 percent to 54 percent.

The five most common grievances reported by computer coordinators were the lack of (1) time and staff, (2) administrative support, (3) teacher interest, (4) budget, and (5) additional compensation and appreciation.

Effect on Formal Education

Computer use may assist in breaking down barriers between formal and informal education. According to Friedrichs and Schaff, even though social interaction will continue to play a major part in the educational process, learning at home may become an increasingly important feature of the educational system (31). This idea is already a reality in developments such as the British Open University, which combines home study with summer school sessions that emphasize social interaction. The same authors caution that social interaction is not the only learning area where the computer is an inadequate substitute for the human teacher. Knowledge and information are not necessarily synonymous terms; translating information into a framework of knowledge "requires more complex abilities than mere straightforward transmission" (31, p. 107). Therefore the computer will probably perform better as a tool for the teacher than as a substitute.

After extensive investigations, Gleason (33) made several observations and predictions that illustrate both the challenges and the opportunities for education that have emerged, in large part, as a result of the computer and its potential uses. As educators plan for the future it is well to keep them in mind. Although these observations were made in 1981, they seem just as appropriate today. They include the following:

1. Dramatic and exciting developments in communications hardware of all types will continue to emerge. Technological developments will remain far ahead of actual application. Schools will work at implementing new technology but will lag behind most other societal institutions.
2. Skills in computer operation will become more a part of the "basics" of education as the computer moves into the home and becomes increasingly important in the industrial world.
3. Neighborhood and home-based learning centers will provide much of the instruction now provided by the school. Pressure for accountability and competency "will shift from the schools to the individual and possibly to the family."
4. As schools are relieved of some of the burden of teaching content, educators should be able to concentrate more on social interaction, value development, creative thinking, and other objectives now being pushed aside by the back-to-basics movement. While computers will not replace teachers, they may change their role to that of "planning and providing those higher-order learning experiences that cannot be provided by technological devices."
5. The entire concept of learning will undergo a gradual but significant change. "Learning will be living, not just what you do in school." (33, pp. 17–18)

Information from "Visions of the Future" (101) seems appropriate here. Items on the wish list of 15 prominent educators included a computerized world library, with home and school access; a telephone and copy machine in every classroom; a computer at each desk; solar-powered laptop; large-screen projection capabilities in each classroom to allow the computer to be used as a replacement for the chalkboard; and classroom teleconferencing capabilities, bringing authors, scientists, and other people to the classroom without having to travel great distances, and bringing students face to face with other students all over the world. One person suggested that the most important obstacle is not a lack of better materials, but providing teachers with more skills in using current resources more effectively and in accurately assessing student learning. Another stated that what teachers need most is an "aware heart."

CONCLUSION

Educational computing is only a little more than 30 years old (72). In just three decades, the computer has won a respected position in the classrooms of America and around the world. It presents issues and poses questions far too numerous and complex to treat comprehensively within these few pages. This monograph describes the current status of educational computing as presented in current literature and discusses some of the issues and concerns currently faced by those who are using the computer as an educational tool. Issues not dealt with herein are laptop computers, distance learning, and electronic mail, to name but a few. Many others are treated very briefly, with references provided for further study.

Computer research already reported in the field of education is encouraging, and the results are generally positive. Schools are welcoming the new technology with a rather high level of enthusiasm, even though implementation lags behind industry, medicine, and other fields. Students are motivated and maintain interest over sustained periods of time. As hardware becomes still more powerful and abundant, it is reasonable to expect increased educational benefits and continued positive reactions from students and teachers. Acceptance and effectiveness of new technology and software are reflected in the improved videodisc and its momentum of success in the schools today.

Despite these encouraging indicators, however, computer use in the schools is not without its problems. The increased efforts of both producers and users are needed to ensure the availability of quality software. There must be careful research before mass production and quality control during the production process. Additionally, guidelines for software protection must be clear and they must be respected.

The roles of the computer in the relationship between education and industry are barely identified, but already they indicate far-reaching potential. Computer use in teacher training and its effect on formal education will likely prove both beneficial and frustrating as future developments materialize.

Another concern directly related to the subject of this monograph is the kind and quality of research conducted. Care must be taken so that the results will be accurate and useful.

Although the new technology staggers the imagination and offers exciting opportunities, it is well to remember that it offers no guarantees. The computer is only a tool; educators must face the challenge of using its full potential. People are still in control and will determine its use. Therein lies the opportunity as well as the challenge.

BIBLIOGRAPHY

1. Allred, Ruel A. *Spelling: The Application of Research Findings.* Washington, D.C.: National Education Association, 1977. p. 35.
2. Bailey, Zan Tamar. "CAI and Interactive Video Enhance Students' Scores on the College Level Academic Skills Test." *Technological Horizons in Education* (September 1990): 82–85.
3. Baker, Frank B.; Ratanakesdatan, Peeropong; and McIsaac, Donald N. "A Micro-Computer Based Test Scoring System." *Educational Technology* (February 1978): 36–39.
4. Balajthy, Ernest. *Computers and Reading: Lessons from the Past and the Technologies of the Future.* Englewood Cliffs, N.J.: Prentice-Hall, 1989.
5. Becker, Henry J. "Computer Use in United States Schools: 1989. An Initial Report of U.S. Participation in the I.E.A. Computers in Education Survey." Paper presented at the meetings of the American Educational Research Association, September 1990.
6. Becker, Henry Jay. *Microcomputers in the Classroom: Dreams and Realities.* Eugene, Ore.: International Council for Computers in Education, 1983.
7. Bitter, Gary G., and Camuse, Ruth A. *Using a Microcomputer in the Classroom.* Englewood Cliffs, N.J.: Prentice-Hall, 1988.
8. Bleed, Ron. "Natural Language System Tracks High School Students At Risk." *Technological Horizons In Education* (September 1990): 77–78.
9. Block, Karen K.; Tucker, Shirley A.: and Butler, Patricia A. *Spelling Learning and Retention Under Variations in Focal Unit of Word Presentation in Computer-Assisted Spelling Drill.* Report No. PU-LRDC-1974-3. Pittsburgh: University of Pittsburgh, Pennsylvania Learning Research and Development Center, 1974.
10. Bradley, Virginia N. "Improving Students' Writing with Microcomputers." *Language Arts* (October 1982): 732–38.
11. Bright, George W. *Microcomputer Applications.* Newton, Mass.: Allyn and Bacon, 1987.
12. Brooks, Susan. "Using Application Software with Gifted Students." *Computing Teacher* (November 1990): 41–43.
13. Brown, Betty. "PLATO Promises Grade Gains." *Electronic Education* (October 1981): 10–12.
14. Bruder, Isabelle. "Future Teachers: Are They Prepared?" *Electronic Learning* (January/February 1989): 32–39.
15. Bruder, Isabelle. "The Third Computer Coordinator Survey." *Electronic Learning* (April 1990): 24–29.
16. Bruwelheide, Janis H. "Teacher Competencies for Microcomputer Use in the Classroom: A Literature Review." *Educational Technology* (October 1982): 29–31.
17. Bukoski, William J., and Korotkin, Arthur L. "Computing Activities in Secondary Education." *Educational Technology* (January 1976): 9–23.
18. Burns, Patricia Knight, and Bozeman, William C. "Computer-Assisted Instruction and Mathematics Achievement: Is There a Relationship?" *Educational Technology* (October 1981): 32–39.
19. Burroughs, Robert. "New Teaching, New Learning." *Electronic Learning* (January 1990): 2–16.
20. Carman, Gary O., and Kosberg, Bernard. "Educational Technology Research: Computer Technology and the Education of Emotionally Handicapped Children." *Educational Technology* (February 1982): 26–30.
21. Cates, Ward Mitchell. "Research Findings Applied to Software Design: Computerized Instructional Spelling Programs." *Journal of Computer-Based Instruction,* 16, no. 1 (Winter 1989): 36–45.

22. Clement, Frank J. "Affective Considerations in Computer-Based Education." *Educational Technology* (April 1981): 228–32.
23. Crouse, David B. "The Computerized Gradebook as a Component of a Computer-Managed Curriculum." *Educational Technology* (May 1981): 16–20.
24. Davis, Robert B. "Alternative Uses of Computers in Schools: Cognitive vs. Natural Language Statements." Paper presented at the annual meeting of the American Educational Research Association, Boston, April 7–11, 1980. ED 184 885.
25. Demshock, George M., and Riedesel, C. Alan. *Use of C.A.I. to Teach Spelling to Sixth Graders: Final Report.* University Park: Pennsylvania State University, August 1968.
26. Denny, Charles F., and Denny, Glenda W. "Spoonful of Science." *Science and Children* (May 1990): 16–17.
27. Engel, F. L., and Andriessen, J. J. "Educational Technology Research: Computer-Aided Learning of a Foreign Vocabulary." *Educational Technology* (May 1981): 46–53.
28. Fey, Thomas Frederick. "A Comparison of Computer and Teacher-Prepared Individualized Reading Prescriptions." Doctoral dissertation, University of Florida, 1975. *Dissertation Abstracts International,* 1976, 36, 5222A–23A. (University Microfilms No. 76–4231)
29. Fishman, Elizabeth Jane; Keller, Leo; and Atkinson, Richard C. "Masses vs. Distributed Practice in Computerized Spelling Drills." *Journal of Educational Psychology,* 59, no. 4 (August 1968): 290–96.
30. Frantz, Nevin R., Jr. "The Development and Field Testing of a Computer-Managed Delivery System for Individualizing Instruction in Multioccupational Programs for Vocational Education: Final Report." Research Report, April 1978. ED 146 445.
31. Friedrichs, Buenter, and Schaff, Adam. *Microelectronics and Society: A Report to the Club of Rome.* New York: Mentor, 1983.
32. Gershman, Janis, and Sakamoto, Evannah. "Computer-Assisted Remediation and Evaluation: A CAI Project for Ontario Secondary Schools." *Educational Technology* (March 1981): 40–43.
33. Gleason, Gerald T. "Microcomputers in Education: The State of the Art." *Educational Technology* (March 1981): 7–18.
34. Glenn, Allen D., and Kehrberg, Kent T. "The Intelligent Videodisc: An Instructional Tool for the Classroom." *Educational Technology* (October 1981): 60–63.
35. Goldberg, Kenneth P. "Bringing Mathematics to the Social Studies Class: Spreadsheets and the Electoral Process." *Computing Teacher* (August/September 1990): 35–38.
36. Grabe, Mark, and Grabe, Cindy. "The Microcomputer and the Language Experience Approach." *Reading Teacher,* 38, no. 6 (February 1985): 508–11.
37. Greenman, Mark D. "A Computer-Based Problem Solving Geography Unit." *Computing Teacher* (October 1990): 22–23.
38. Grossnickle, Donald R.; Larid, Bruce A.; Cutter, Thomas W.; and Tefft, James A. "Profile of Change in Education: A High School Faculty Adopts/Rejects Microcomputers." *Educational Technology* (June 1982): 17–19.
39. Hall, M. "The Case for Computerized Instuctional Management." *Educational Technology* (June 1988): 34–37.
40. Harper, Dennis O., and Stewart, James H. *Run: Computer Education.* Monterey, Calif.: Brooks/Cole Publishing Co., 1983.
41. Hasselbring, Ted S. "Remediating Spelling Problems of Learning-Handicapped Students Through the Use of Microcomputers." *Educational Technology* (April 1982): 31–32.
42. Hasselbring, Ted S., and Crossland, Cathy L. "Using Microcomputers for Diagnosing Spelling Problems in Learning-Handicapped Children." *Educational Technology* (April 1981): 37–39.

43. Hasselbring, Ted S., and Goin, Laura I. "Use of Computers." In *Best Practices in Mental Disabilities,* vol. 2, edited by Greg A. Robinsin and others, ch. 8, 1988. ED 304 838.
44. Hativa, N. "CAI Versus Paper and Pencil: Discrepancies in Students' Performance." *Instructional Science* 17 (1988): 77–79.
45. Hawkridge, David. "Who Needs Computers in Schools, and Why?" *Computers in Education,* 15, no. 1–3 (1990): 1–6.
46. Herrmann, Andrea W. "Teaching Writing with Computers: Are We Being Realistic?" Paper presented at the annual meeting of South Central Modern Language Association, Houston, Texas, October 29–31, 1987. ED 288 199.
47. Hoffman, Jeffery L., and Waters, Keith. "Some Effects of Student Personality on Success with Computer-Assisted Instruction." *Educational Technology* (March 1982): 20–21.
48. Hoffman, Karen I., and Lundberg, George D. "A Comparison of Computer-Monitored Group Tests with Paper-and-Pencil Tests." *Educational and Psychological Measurement* (1976): 791–809.
49. Holden, Constance. "Computers Make Slow Progress in Class." *Science* (May 26, 1989): 906–9.
50. Holz, Else, and others. "Computer-Assisted Instruction for Teaching Basic Money Handling Skills to Mentally Handicapped Students at Christine Meikle School in Calgary." Research Report, June 1982. ED 212 101.
51. Hoover, Todd, and Gould, Sandra. "The Pirating of Computer Programs: A Survey of Software Producers." *Educational Technology* (October 1982): 23–26.
52. "In the News: Networked." *Science and Children* (May 1990): 8–9.
53. Jenkins, Tracie M., and Dankert, Elizabeth J. "Results of a Three-Month PLATO Trial in Terms of Utilization and Student Attitudes." *Educational Technology* (March 1981): 44–47.
54. Jolicoeur, Karen, and Berger, Dale E. "Implementing Educational Software and Evaluating Its Academic Effectiveness: Part I." *Educational Technology* (Sept. 1988): 7–19.
55. Kibler, Tom R., and Campbell, Patricia B. "Reading, Writing and Computing: Skills of the Future." *Educational Technology* (September 1976): 44–46.
56. Knight, Carlton W. II, and Dunglebeger, Gary E. "The Influence of Computer-Managed Self-Paced Instruction on Science Attitudes of Students." *Journal of Research in Science Teaching,* 14, no. 6 (1977): 551–55.
57. Knutson, J.M. *Spelling Drills Using a Computer-Assisted Instructional System.* Technical Report No. 112. Stanford, Calif.: Institute for Mathematical Studies in the Social Sciences, Stanford University, 1967.
58. Kochan, Barbara. "How to Handle Children's Spelling Mistakes on the Microcomputer?" *Education and Computing,* 3, nos. 3–4 (1987): 219–22.
59. Korotkin, Arthur L., and others. "A Study of the Use of Computers in the Development of Science Career Awareness in Elementary School Children." Research Report, April 1979. ED 162 894.
60. Kraus, William H. "Using a Computer Game to Reinforce Skills in Addition Basic Facts in Second Grade." *Journal for Research in Mathematics Education* (March 1981): 152–55.
61. Lally, M. "Computer-Assisted Development of Number Conservation in Mentally Retarded School Children." *Australian Journal of Developmental Disabilities* (September 1980): 131–36.
62. Litchfield, Brenda C. "Slipping a Disk in the Classroom: The Latest in Video Technology." *Science and Children* (September 1990): 16–21.

63. MacArthur, Charles A. "The Impact of Computers on the Writing Process." *Exceptional Children,* 54, no. 6 (April 1988): 536–42.
64. MacLean, Robert Frederick. "A Comparison of Three Methods of Presenting Instruction in Introductory Multiplication to Elementary School Children (total computer, partial computer, and non-computer)." Doctoral dissertation, Temple University, 1974. *Dissertation Abstracts International,* 1974, 35, 1430A. (University Microfilms No. 74–19, 759)
65. Mageau, Therese. "Software's New Frontier: Laser-Disk Technology." *Electronic Learning* (March 1990): 22–28.
66. Malone, T. W. "Toward a Theory of Instrinsically Motivating Instruction." *Cognitive Science* 4 (1981): 333–69.
67. Martin, Joan; Chiu, Mai-Hung; and Dailey, Anne. "Graphing in the Second Grade." *Computing Teacher* (November 1990): 28–32.
68. Maser, Arthur L., and others. "Highline Public Schools Computer-Assisted Instruction Project: A Program to Meet Disadvantaged Students; Individual Needs for Basic Skill Development: Final Report." Research Report, July 1979. ED 167 114.
69. McCarthy, Robert. "The New Library/Media Center." *Electronic Learning* (May/June 1990): 25–28.
70. McMillan, Gordon. "Multimedia: An Educator's Link to the 90s." *Computing Teacher* (November 1990): 7–9.
71. Merrill, David M.; Schneider, Edward W.; and Fletcher, Kathie A. *TICCIT.* Englewood Cliffs, N.J.: Educational Technology Publications, 1980.
72. Molnar, Andrew R. "Computers in Education: A Historical Perspective of the Unfinished Task." *Technological Horizons in Education* (November 1990): 80–83.
73. Molnar, Andrew R. "The Coming of Computer Literacy: Are We Prepared for It?" *Educational Technology* (January 1981): 26–28.
74. Morgan, Catherine E., and others. "Evaluation of Computer-Assisted Instruction, 1975-76." Research Report, October 1977. ED 139 655.
75. Moursund, David. *Teacher's Guide to Computers in the Elementary School.* Eugene, Ore.: International Council for Computers in Education, 1980.
76. Naiman, Adeline. "A Hard Look at Educational Software." *BYTE* (February 1987): 193–200.
77. Nathan, Joe. "Viewpoint: Fighting School-Computer Fad." *Info World,* July 25, 1983.
78. National Council of Teachers of Mathematics. *An Agenda for Action.* Reston, Va.: The Council, 1980.
79. National Education Association. *A Teacher Survey NEA Report: Computers in the Classroom.* Washington, D.C.: The Association, 1983.
80. Newman, D., and others. "Computer Mediation of Collaborative Science Investigations." *Journal of Educational Computing Research,* 5, no. 2 (1989): 151–66.
81. Nieminen, Gayla, and others. "Computers in Education. Hinsdale District #181. 1986-87 Update." ED 309 765.
82. Niess, Margaret L. "Preparing Computer Using Educators in a New Decade." *Computing Teacher* (November 1990): 10+.
83. Outhred, Lynne. "Word Processing: Its Impact on Children's Writing." *Journal of Learning Disabilities,* 22, no. 4 (April 1989): 262–64.
84. Paske, Richard. "Hypermedia: A Progress Report Part 3: CD-ROM, CD-I, DVI, Etc." *Technological Horizons in Education* (October 1990): 93–97.
85. Patterson, Jerry L.; Drifke, James; and Fox, Ron F. "Computerized Report Cards." *Educational Technology* (August 1976): 39–42.
86. Pollack, Harvey. "Computer-Simulated Laboratory (CSL): Rationale and Approaches to the Structuring of CSL Exercises." *Educational Technology* (March 1976): 39–42.
87. Portwood, G.; Elliott, L.; and Nelsen, R. *Where in Time Is Carmen San Diego?* San Rafael, Calif.: Broderbund, 1989.

88. Reisman, Sorel, and Swanson, Curtis W. "The Trials and Triumphs of Interactive Videodisc at a Traditional University." *Technological Horizons in Education* (October 1990): 72–74.
89. Robertson, Gladene. *A Comparison of Meaningful and Nonmeaningful Content in Computer-Assisted Spelling Programs.* Saskatchewan, Canada: Saskatchewan School Trustees Association Research Center, 1978.
90. Robinett, W. *Rocky's Boots.* Menlo Park, Calif.: Learning Co., 1982.
91. Roecks, Alan L., and Chapin, John. "Mathematics Achievement in Schools Having and Not Having CMI: An Assessment of MICA." Paper presented at the annual meeting of the American Educational Research Association, New York, April 1977. ED 142 393.
92. Roth, Wolff-Michael. "Experimenting with Temperature Probes." *Science and Children* (November/December 1989): 52–54.
93. Saltinski, Ronald. "Microcomputers in Social Studies: An Innovative Technology for Instruction." *Educational Technology* (January 1981): 29–32.
94. Saracho, Olivia N. "The Effects of a Computer-Assisted Instruction Program on Basic Skills Achievement and Attitudes Toward Instruction of Spanish-Speaking Migrant Children." *American Educational Research Journal* (Summer 1982): 201–19.
95. Scanland, W. "Computer-Managed Instruction-Navy Style." *Campus* (December 1975): 25–27.
96. Schmid, Jon. "Survey of Computer Use in Missouri Social Science Classrooms Reveals Problems and Promise." *Technological Horizons in Education* (October 1990): 86–89.
97. Schneider, E. W. "Videodiscs, or the Individualization of Instructional Television." *Education Technology* (May 1976): 53–58.
98. Schwartz, Mimi. "Computers and the Teaching of Writing." *Educational Technology* (November 1982): 27–29.
99. Smith, Nancy J. "The Word Processing Approach to Language Experience." *Reading Teacher*, 38 (February 1985): 556–59.
100. Sorlie, William E.; Essec, Diane; and Shatzer, John. "Computer Automated from Sign-on to Item Analysis: A Student Appraisal System." *Educational Technology* (November 1979): 29–34.
101. Steele, Eileen. "Visions of the Future." *Electronic Learning* (January 1990): 24–30.
102. Steele, Kathleen J.; Battista, Michael T.; and Krockover, Gerald H. "The Effect of Microcomputer Assisted Instruction upon the Computer Literacy of High-Ability Students." *Gifted Child Quarterly* (Fall 1982): 162–64.
103. Strickland, Dorothy S.; Feeley, Joan T.; and Wepner, Shelley B. *Using Computers in the Teaching of Reading.* New York: Teachers College, Columbia University, 1987.
104. "Technology and the At-Risk Student." *Electronic Learning* (November/December 1988): 35–49.
105. Teulings, Hans-Leo H. M., and Thomassen, Arnold J. W. M. "Computer-Aided Analysis of Handwriting Movements." *Visible Language,* 13, no. 3 (1981): 218–31. ED 223 508.
106. Tsai, San-Yun W., and Pohl, Norval F. "Student Achievement in Computer Programming: Lecture vs. Computer-Aided Instruction." *Journal of Experimental Education* (Winter 1977): 66–70.
107. Van Hess, E. J. W. M. "Computer-Managed Learning at the University Level in the Netherlands." *Educational Technology* (April 1976): 28–31.
108. Wall, Shavaun M., and Taylor, Nancy E. "Using Interactive Computer Programs in Teaching Higher Conceptual Skills: An Approach to Instruction in Writing." *Educational Technology* (February 1982): 13–17.

109. Watkins, Marley W., and Webb, Cynthia. "Computer-Assisted Intruction with Learning-Disabled Students." *Educational Computer* (September/October 1981): 24–27.
110. Weaver, Phyllis A., and others. "Perceptual Units Training for Improving Word Analysis Skills." Technical Report No. 1. Research Report, March 1982. ED 219 739.
111. Weiland, Barbara. "Disc-over Visual Learning." *Science and Children* (September 1990): 22–23.
112. Wepner, Shelley B. "Holistic Computer Applications in Literature-Based Classrooms." *Reading Teacher*, 44, no. 1 (September 1990): 12–19.
113. Wepner, Shelley B. "Stepping Forward with Reading Software." *Reading, Writing, and Learning Disabilities*, 5 (1989): 61–83.
114. Woodruff, Earl; Bereiter, Carl; and Scardamalia, Marlene. "On the Road to Computer-Assisted Compositions." *Journal of Educational Technology Systems*, 10, no. 2 (1981): 133–48.
115. Wright, E. B., and Forcier, R. C. *The Computer: A Tool for the Teacher.* Belmont, Calif.: Wadsworth, 1985.